God is Up to Something!

Jose and Angela Vargas

God is Up to Something!

Copyright©2023 by Jose and Angela Vargas

All rights reserved.

Scripture quotations marked "NKJV" are taken from the New King James Version. Copyright © 1982 by Thomas Nelson, Inc. Used by permission. All rights reserved. Bible text from the New King James Version® is not to be reproduced in copies or otherwise by any means except as permitted in writing by Thomas Nelson, Inc., Attn: Bible Rights and Permissions, P.O. Box 141000, Nashville, TN 37214-1000.

ISBN: 9798388287595

DEDICATION

We want to dedicate this book to our children Kianna, Jose Jr., and Marisol and to our grandson Josiah. Thank you for supporting us and for encouraging us. Thank you for being with us through the ups and downs. We pray that our story would be an example to each of you that God is faithful and that Anything is possible with God! Always remember this; God first, family second, and ministry third. We love you and never forget that God is Up To Something!

Love Always,
Dad and Mom

Contents

DEDICATION 1

FOREWORD 3

INTRODUCTION 4

CHAPTER 1 5

CHAPTER 2 20

CHAPTER 3 40

CHAPTER 4 47

CHAPTER 5 55

CHAPTER 6 63

CHAPTER 7 72

CHAPTER 8 79

FOREWORD

We met Angela and Jose when our family relocated to the United States over two decades ago. We met at church in Kansas and our families became fast friends. We moved out of the state of Kansas a few years later, but our families have maintained a very close relationship ever since.

We have walked closely with both of them, and we know that they genuinely love the Lord Jesus.

Angela's testimony is a testament of the redeeming power of Jesus Christ. Hers is a life changed and transformed by the Lord. Jose's testimony is evidence of God's faithfulness and commitment to His children.

Angela fears God and it is evident in so many areas of her life. She is sold out to Jesus, and at the same time humbled that she could be used by Him. Jose is a loyal man and is always careful to make sure his family stays in God's will.

As they have walked through many seasons of life and ministry, they have allowed God to be glorified in many difficult situations rather than let the devil win. In good times and challenging times, they have constantly run to the Lord, and are always willing to learn from others.

Their book is a long-awaited one and we have no doubt that it will bless many lives. Our prayer is that many people will come to know Christ and surrender completely to Him as they read this book.

Dearest Angela and Jose, the Lord is fulfilling His promises in your lives, and we know that His name will be glorified everywhere your book gets to.

Your forever friends,
Emmanuel and Toyin John

INTRODUCTION

"For I know the thoughts that I think towards you…"
Jeremiah 29:11

You know, before the very foundations of the world, God had a plan for our lives. He brought the two of us together to be a team that would serve Him and bring Him glory. He knew that we would go through trials and tribulations, dangers seen and unseen. He also knew that through it all, we would continue to preach His Word and reach the lost.

In our book, *God is Up to Something!* you will hear our testimony of how we learned to live our lives surrendered to God. You will learn how we leaned on the Lord and how we learned how to be open to listen to Him and follow His Will for our lives through our journeys, from our early lives to our life as a married couple, as parents, and pastors.

It is our sincere prayer that as you read this book, it will draw you deep into the heart of God and that you will want to have an even deeper relationship with Him. We give God all the glory for what He has done…
And as we always say…
"God is Up to Something!"

CHAPTER 1
Angela

Wow, how do I begin telling my story? I think that I'll just start at the beginning.

I grew up in a single parent home with my mom and seven siblings in Greensboro, GA, a city that is located on the outskirts of Atlanta, GA. I have 4 sisters and 2 brothers. We lived in a low-income apartment complex, like the projects. It was a place where there were mostly moms raising kids— no dads in the homes. It was one of those kinds of neighborhoods where everybody knew everybody.

My mom worked hard to make sure we had what we needed. As a matter of fact, she worked two jobs for as long as I can remember. She was always working.

Because my mom was always gone because of her work, we used to go outside and play a lot. I have so many memories of those days!

I remember the times when we would go to our aunt and uncle's houses. I was 6 years old when we were at her house picking fruit and doing a lot of gardening. As I grew older, I would hang out with my cousins. All of us lived in the same neighborhood, so we went from house to house playing with each other on a daily basis. We would play all kinds of games.

We played Hide and Go Seek, football, and even twirled our hoola hoops. As time went by, we began to develop friendships with other kids in the neighborhood.

I remember the nights when I would lay down on the sidewalk and look up at the stars when I was 8 years old.

My sisters and I would count the stars for hours, but we could never ever finish counting them.

I used to say, "There's something in the sky."

As I looked up into the dark night sky, there always seemed to be one star that shone a little brighter than the others.

We would draw pictures of the stars and sometimes we would get our chalk and draw stars and even the moon on the sidewalk.

Soon our joy of starwatching would bring us back to reality, as our mom would call out to us to come inside for dinner. It was now time for us to wash our hands and take a shower. We would then gather as a family to eat dinner.

Mom would make hot water corn bread, soup, collard greens, chicken, and mashed potatoes. We had a feast for every meal.

As time went on, I began to develop into who I was becoming. I was just 10 years old, but I was maturing early because my mom worked so much. I was the oldest girl, so I had to take care of my siblings.

Time went on. I was now babysitting when I was 11. Then, when I was 12 years old, I started cooking full course meals. I was wearing several hats at this time of my life. I was the cook and helped my siblings with homework because my mom was working.

We had created a schedule of weekly duties in our household. Every Saturday I did the groceries and laundry. Me and three of my siblings (the one next to the oldest and the third to the oldest) would walk to the grocery store. Then we would bring the groceries home and put them away. Sunday was our cleaning day.

Our family didn't take vacations. Our vacations consisted of going from Greensboro to Atlanta to see my aunt and uncle.

Atlanta was my summer vacation—my vacation from home. My mom was always working, so she couldn't take all of us on vacation. So, a lot of my time was spent at home.

At the age of 14, I was getting involved in sports in school. I stayed after school and ran track. At the time we didn't have a car, so I would walk home after every meet. Then I would cook, iron clothes, help my siblings with homework, run their bath water, and start all over again.

Sometimes I would get home late after some of my sports activities. In those instances, my aunt came to the rescue. She lived close to us, so she was able to step in and help with the cooking, doing my siblings' hair and getting the groceries.

A few years later I got a job at a fast-food restaurant. I was about 15 or 16 years old at the time.

I got the job, then learned that my sister (who was 15 at the time) was pregnant. Some family members wanted her to have an abortion, but I told her not to. I told her that I would quit everything to take care of the baby. So now, in addition to working, I found myself taking care of a brand-new baby (my niece), taking care of my siblings, trying to do sports, and going to school. I was doing a whole lot. But before I knew it, another surprise was waiting for me— just around the corner.

When I turned 17, things began to change for me. It was October when I met Jose (my future husband) at a football game. He was in the military and would travel to Georgia on the weekends. Because I was the oldest child in the family and taking care of everybody and everything, she didn't allow me to date.

However, we started a long-distance dating relationship. Jose was stationed in North Carolina, but he would come to see me every weekend.

He would come every weekend, but I could only see him for two days. Then he would head back to the Marine Corps base.

Now, Jose was 20 years old and, because he was in the Marine Corps, couldn't date anyone younger than 18.

So, I lied and told him I was 18. I was actually 17.

Well, November rolled around, and it was time for my birthday party. My mom got me a cake. Jose came to the party too, and boy was he shocked to learn that I had JUST turned 18!

Now it was December, and just before Christmas, Jose asked my mom if he could marry me. We had only known each other for a few months and now he was asking my mom for my hand in marriage…

My mom told him that it was fine with her if he wanted to marry me. So, on Christmas Eve, he proposed to me—with the ring! And I said YES!

So, he leaves and goes back to North Carolina that Sunday night, and for that whole week he was working.

Then he returned the following weekend and said, "Let's get married soon, so you can come back with me."

So, instead of getting married in July, we moved the date up to February 5, 1994.

After we got married, I immediately left for Camp Lejeune in North Carolina. I left my siblings behind. It was one of the hardest things that I had to do.

Time moved on and now I found myself wearing a new hat in a new season of my life. I was now a married woman. But even though I was married, I was still concerned about my siblings.

I thought about them, and I wondered who would take care of them since I was no longer there.

After moving to Jacksonville, North Carolina, I would go every other weekend to Greensboro to visit my family back in Georgia. I would still be bringing siblings with me during the week and weekend!

During the first few years of our marriage, the house was always kept clean, and the meals were always prepared because this was how I always did it when I was 12.

I had already been taught how to do that.

I got pregnant right away after I got married. During my ninth month of pregnancy, Jose got deployed. I was there alone in North Carolina, so my mom asked me to transfer everything to Georgia so she could help me with the baby.

So, I went back to Georgia and gave birth to Kianna, a beautiful baby girl at Minnie G Boswell Hospital in Greensboro.

It was a complicated birth—36 hours. Not only was it a complicated birth, but I also ended up getting an infection. So, they had to do an emergency C-section. Jose made it back to Georgia right before it was done.

After the baby was born, I stayed with my mom for about 6 to 8 weeks so that I could heal before I went back to North Carolina.

The Accident

It was a late night when we found ourselves heading back home from Greensboro to North Carolina. We were heading home with our sweet little Kianna. There she was sitting all cozy in her car seat, with my cousin and sister sitting on the back seat next to her.

All seemed to be right with the world—at least we thought it was at the time. But what would happen on this night would be something that we would never, ever forget.

As the car headed down the road, fog rolled over the night sky. Suddenly, a deer jumped out in front of the car. Jose quickly swerved the car. The car went soaring a full 360° on its side. Then it went backwards and ended up laying sideways in a ditch. Now check this out. I said the car was LAYING SIDEWAYS in a ditch.

BUT NOTHING HAPPENED TO ANY OF US!

Not a scratch! Not a broken bone! Not a single injury—to anybody!

As a matter of fact, when I looked back to see if my baby was okay, she was still strapped in her car seat! She had pooped in her diaper and was laughing. It was the strangest experience!

After everything calmed down a bit, we called the tow

truck to get us out. Now the car was pretty banged up. It was all mashed in on one side, but it was still drivable. So, we headed down the road again. We drove about 4 miles. Guess what happened?

We ended up with two flat tires! Now we had to wait inside the car, while Jose walked a long way to a fellow Marine's home, then to our home to get two spare tires. Then he drove him back so he could put the tires on our car. We did eventually make it home.

Tougher Times

Kianna ended up catching pneumonia. Jose was home the day we took her to the hospital, then the next day he was deployed. They had an IV in her head, and one in her foot. It was such a tough time for me.

There I was, at the hospital for a week, with our baby in the ICU. I had no car, no family, my husband was on deployment, hadn't eaten, and had no sleep. I was freaking out, and scared.

Soon, Kianna recovered and was released from the hospital. Jose got back from deployment a couple of days later. Then he was deployed for the next year and a half, which left me raising Kianna by myself.

Living a military lifestyle was very hard for me. I was married and only 19 years old, so having a husband who was in the military left me alone— a lot.

I almost felt like I was living in the same cycle as my mom who was left to raise us alone.

Because of this, I was harboring a lot of internal anger. I held resentment on the inside.

Now for the next year and a half, life around the house was pretty normal. But I was still missing my family, so I visited them every other weekend, staying connected with them while Jose was deployed.

Shortly after he re-enlisted, we got orders to go to Hawaii. We were stationed at the Marine Corps base in Kaneohe Bay, Hawaii. My brother came to visit me in Hawaii, but the rest of my family could not.

We were super excited about this move. It was like a dream come true for me to go to Hawaii!

Once we arrived and were settled in Hawaii, things began to change for me. I started hanging out with some of the military wives. Now, I had met some friends on the base and started going out with them. I started partying with them because my husband was gone a lot.

Some friends on the base watched my daughter while I went out, and so did my brother, (after getting into some trouble while he was back in Georgia) who had moved in with us. So, the babysitting was all covered.

I was working during the week, but I would hit the clubs on the weekends. I was doing this cycle for a period of time. Since Jose was always deployed and gone so much, going out seemed to help me with the stress and anxiety that I was feeling inside. Then something else hit me that shook me to my core. While I was in Hawaii, I went through losing my best friend from high school, and then my grandmother. Because Hawaii was so far, and we weren't making a lot of money in the military, I couldn't make it to my friend's funeral, but I did make it to my grandmother's funeral. I took Kianna with me, and Jose stayed behind.

For Better or Worse...

It was during the time that I went to my grandmother's funeral...

THAT'S when things really started going downhill for me. Jose had returned home from deployment, and I went back to work.

Things got real bad. It was during this time that I had been hearing some things through the grapevine. I had found out that there was some adultery going on. I found this out through other people, but not from my husband.

Now I am real angry and upset. I'm trying to find out what in the world is going on.

Let me tell you how it all started...

I was at work one day, just minding my own business, when a guy came to my job.

He said, "I heard that your husband had committed adultery with my wife."

Then I said, "Okay, thank you."

After hearing this, I left work, and walked home. I was anxious and mad. I was so mad that I left my keys behind. But I didn't go back to get them. I was so mad that I ran to my house. When I got there, I busted out the glass window with my fist. Glass shattered and there was blood all over my hand and on the back door.

Once I got inside, I grabbed my machete knife. Then I called up a friend on base and I asked him to "Please take me to Jose's job."

So, we pull up to his job. I got out of the car, walking with no shoes on and holding the machete in my hand.

Suddenly, Jose's friend ran in front of me, to beat me to Jose first. Once he caught up with him, he told him that I was out there with the machete.

Just then Jose's staff NCOIC (noncommissioned officer in charge) ran outside to me and told me that I had to put the knife up and leave.

I said, "I'm not going nowhere until I talk to Sergeant Vargas!"

Then he told me that if I didn't leave the premises, they would call the MP (military police).

After he said that, Jose told me we would talk about it later when he got home. So, his friend took me back home.

Well—almost home.

Actually, he drove me down the street to the lady's house (the one that I was told Jose committed adultery with).

I got out of the car with my machete, then knocked on her front door.

I said, "Open up!"

Then she asked, "Who is this?"

I replied, "This is Angela and I need to talk to you!"

She answered, "I already know what you are coming down here for."

Because her husband had already told her that he had gone to my job to tell me that she was cheating with my husband.

At that point, instead of opening the door, she just kept yelling. Finally, she came to the front window and opened the blinds and just stood there, looking at me.

So, I told her, "I am going to cut you up with my knife!"

I was so angry. I kept pursuing. I was kicking the door trying to get inside. By this time, she picks up the phone and calls the cops on me.

Jose's friend then gets in the car and says, "Let's go! She's calling the cops!"

Then we left. But something on the inside of me kept telling me they both were lying to me.

Later on, the daycare worker dropped Kiki off at home.

Jose came home afterwards. Once he walked in the door, I asked him if it was true. He denied the whole thing. But I was still mad.

The argument kept going on and on. Tempers flared, and that's when I told him…

"If you stay here tonight and go to sleep, I am going to LIGHT YOU UP and SET YOU ON FIRE!"

After hearing those words, he decided to go for a run.

When he came back from his run, he called his staff NCOIC and told him what had happened. A few minutes later, he pulled up to the house and told Jose that he had to go with him.

Jose stayed with him for three days at his house until I calmed down. Then he called me on the third day and asked if he could come home. My daughter was crying for him to come home. Because of that, I told him he could come home. I was still angry, and I hated him. But I only let him come back home because of our daughter.

After all of that took place, he would go to work and come back home every day. He would come home and drink and sit outside and smoke every day.

That was his pattern every day. Life was rough at home during this time. We were at home arguing every day about something.

There I was with no family, nobody to talk to, except for those I was partying with. I could have talked to my friend across the street, but she was going through stuff with her own husband, so I couldn't talk to her. I couldn't talk to my family because I didn't want them to know what was going on.

So, there I was, feeling like I was on an island—all alone.

A New Friend

A month later, Jose got deployed to Australia.

It was then that I started going out and started talking to a guy from a different military base. I would go partying on a different side of the island. During this time in my life, I was so angry. After talking to this guy, I liked him. I had started contemplating divorce. I was done with my marriage.

Done, done, done.

I had it all planned out in my head. I wasn't going to work the marriage out.

So, I was talking to the guy and one night, my husband called me. I told him over the phone—while he was deployed in Australia— that when he got back, we were getting a divorce. I told him that I didn't love him and that I didn't want to be with him. Then I told him that I had a new boyfriend. When I told him that, he hung up.

He called me a few days later. That was when he admitted that he had committed adultery. Now he's away from me, so now he comes clean. I'm even madder now because I can't get to him. I am dealing with internal and outward anger.

After hearing this from him, I cursed him out.

Then I told him, "Don't come back here! I'm not picking you up from the airport! I have a new boyfriend!"

After that, Jose came home a month and a half later.

Now the new guy that I was with—that for me was just companionship. It wasn't an intimate relationship.

I was just trying to fill a void…

The void that I had from a father that wasn't in my life...

The void that I had with a husband who had hurt me …

With this guy, I had found someone who would just listen to me. He talked to me, and we even went to the park with my daughter. There was nothing physical that went on with us, but we were getting close.

He was telling me to leave my husband for him. He told me that he would take care of me and my daughter. He told me that he was getting out of the military and moving back to New York. At the moment, that sounded pretty good to me. Now I'm feeling like someone cares about me and my daughter. I have no family. I have nobody. But he was the person I could talk to and run to.

Once Jose came home, I left out of the front door. I told him that I would be back, that I was going to call my mom.

I went to a payphone and was cursing up a storm. I was cursing so bad because of the anger I had inside. The payphone was located next to a house. The lady heard me and all of that cursing. I told my mom that I was going to move back. I told her that I was leaving Hawaii and coming back to Georgia. Then I hung up the phone. After the call I found myself crying and cursing.

As I walked back towards my house a lady named Karen Boone said, "Hey can I talk to you for a minute?"

I said, "What do you need to talk to me about?"

She replied, "First of all, you need to stop cursing because I have little kids around."

Then she said, "I want to tell you that Jesus loves you."

I said to her, "Jesus doesn't love me."

And at that point, I began to share with her what was going on in my life.

As she was talking, I was trying to get away from her—but she kept insisting on telling me that Jesus loved me, and I kept telling her I had to get home. She was persistent in telling me about Jesus.

She then told me, "I will come by and check on you tomorrow if that's okay."

I said, "Yes, that's fine."

From that point, I decided to go to the legal department on Friday to file for divorce. Now the legal department on the military base rarely closes, but on that day, they had the commanding general's inspection taking place, so I was told to come back on Monday.

Little did I know it at the time, but Sunday was on the way. It would be a day where my life would never be the same again.

Sunday came. I got up that morning, got dressed, then told Kianna that we were going to church. I didn't know what church I was going to, just that we were going.

We went to the chapel on base. It was like right down the street from my house, so we walked. Once we got to this chapel, we sat all the way in the back, just me and my daughter.

I listened to the message. Mind you, I didn't grow up in church or anything. I knew there was a God, but I didn't know anything about Jesus.

The pastor finished the sermon and did the altar call.

Then he said, "There is somebody here... The Lord wants to restore your marriage and heal you..."

Immediately I began to think that he was talking to me.

Then, suddenly, my feet got really cold!

He went on to say, "And if that's you, and you want to give your life to the Lord, and you want to accept Jesus, raise your hand."

So, I raised my hand.

He said, "Stand up to your feet and come to the front."

So, I jumped up from my seat and ran to the front.

I said, "I want to know who this Jesus is. You said that Jesus can restore and heal marriages..."

Then I said, "That's me, because I wanted to kill my husband."

They pulled me to the side after the service and talked to me. It was after the service when I gave my life to the Lord. After that, I talked to them and shared what was happening at the house.

The pastor asked for my husband's information, so I gave him the info. I then left and went home.

Jose had barracks duty, so he came home for lunch on that same Sunday.

I told him, "I got saved today. I gave my life to the Lord."

And I said, "I am going to serve Jesus with or without you. But I'd rather serve Him with you."

After I said that, Jose got angry. Then he picked up his beer and left.

CHAPTER 2
Jose

I was raised in church my whole life. I am a pastor's kid, so when I was 4 years old, we moved from Puerto Rico to Chicago, Illinois. My father served as a full-time evangelist with a denomination. In 1978 he took over a church in Kansas City, Kansas, and that's where our life began.

We went to church every day of the week. There were no days off. And during this time of my life, something amazing happened to me.

The call of God came on my life when I was 8 years old. Of course, at that age you don't even know what that means. But there I was.

I preached my first sermon when I was 10 years old. My dad helped me work on that sermon and I remember the night that I was going to preach. It was a Tuesday night. My dad introduced me. Then I walked up on the stage, faced the congregation… And froze.

Now, here I am, 10 years old and the entire congregation is looking at me and I am looking at them. It felt like forever, and there was silence— for a while.

Before I knew it, my dad walked on the stage and put his arm around me.

Then he said, "You got this."

So, for the next 10 minutes I preached on Jonah refusing to obey God and then repenting and returning. I thought it was a 30-minute message, but it was only 10 minutes.

Afterwards my dad gave me a hug and said, "Son, I am proud of you."

From that day until I could remember, I never wanted to preach again.

So, growing up, you see things that parents try to hide from you, but you see how they are treated. Sometimes they were not treated well. That's another reason why I did not want to go in the ministry.

Occasionally guest speakers would come through our

church, and they would prophesy to me about the call of God on my life. They would tell me how I would travel and preach the gospel, and many would get saved, delivered, and healed through my ministry.

Then, when I got home, I would say to God...

"God, find somebody else, because I don't want to preach."

Now, fast forward...

I am at school having fun, playing with some of the kids, and having a fun time. In the meantime, my father had been diagnosed with kidney failure back when we moved to Chicago. I would see my father go to dialysis 3-4 times a week, still pastor a church and travel as an evangelist. Ever since my baby brother was born, my father had been sick. Throughout his entire illness, he just kept on going. He just kept on doing his pastor duties, his father duties, and his husband duties—even during his disability. If you asked me to give the definition of a father, I would tell you...

My dad was the definition of what a father was.

My father passed away when I was in high school. I remember that day as if it were yesterday.

It was a Sunday night and my father had been hospitalized. He asked my mother if I could stay the night with him in the hospital and my mother said no, because I had school on Monday. He was supposed to be released from the hospital on Monday after dialysis.

During this time, I was a student athlete, and we had a football game that day. I was on the field at warmups, and I looked towards the bleachers and saw my brothers sitting there. They looked upset, so I walked over and talked to them. They told me that something was wrong with Dad and that we needed to get to the hospital ASAP.

So, I ran off the field, still wearing my uniform. I told my coaches that I had to get to the hospital. When I got to the hospital, they had all of the family in one room. My dad's doctor came in and told us that he had tried everything he could, but my father had passed.

Now here I am, 16 years old, the oldest male, and wondering, "What happens now?"

I remember asking myself, "Where is God, and why did he take my dad? Of all the sinners in the world, why didn't He take one of them instead of my dad?"

At this time, I was very active in the church, and my brothers and sisters were all on the worship team.

After my father's death, I wanted nothing to do with church, with God, or with people.

I would attend church, but I would not "be in church." My mind just wasn't there. I would pick up extra shifts at work. I would stay late for some extra football and wrestling practices, anything to keep from going to church.

Even after my father passed, guest speakers would come to the church and bring forth confirmation of past prophecies, but they still did not move me. Why? Because the same question would always reign in my mind…

"Why did you have to take my dad?"

There was a void that was inside of me. I would try to fill that void with alcohol and women. I remember once when I was in high school there was senior prank night.

I got home at 2 in the morning, and I was drunk. My mom opened the door for me, and I was so ashamed, scared, and embarrassed that I ran to my room. That was the first time my mom had seen me drunk or even smelling alcohol on me.

I graduated from high school—the first one to graduate in my family. From there, I joined the United States Marine Corps. In the Marine Corps, they tear you down physically, emotionally, and spiritually. Then they build you back up the way they want you to be.

As time went on, I now found myself trying to fill the void that I had inside of me with the Marine Corps.

Early in my career, I deployed a lot. I was promoted quickly in rank. But even with all of that, there was still a void in my heart.

So, I went back to the alcohol and women—plus, I was now adding drugs into my life. I'm in the Marine Corps getting high, getting drunk, and trying to sleep with as many women as I could.

I remember going on a deployment to the Mediterranean. This is during the Bosnia conflict of 93'. We are sitting off the coast of Bosnia— With rounds going down range.

Seeing war will change your perspective of things. I never knew I had this much anger built up in me. At this point, I had not spoken to my mom or my siblings for at least 8 to 10 months. They were worried about me and wondered where I was. They were probably wondering if I was okay or if I was still alive. So, my mom reached out to the Red Cross, and they got a message to me that I had to call my mom.

So, I got to the nearest phone when I was able to and called her. And I tell you, just to hear her voice…It brought so much peace upon me.

But I am still in a war zone thinking, "Am I going to make it home?"

We ended up going to Israel, and while in Israel we got two days of liberty. So, I decided to go on a tour of the Holy Land. I grew up hearing about these places in the Bible, so I wanted to go see them for myself.

A bunch of us went to a bar before the tour began and we started drinking. I was pretty tipsy to say the least. The tour started at the Garden of Gethsemane. The tour guide opens his Bible to the portion of scripture where Jesus is praying at the Garden of Gethsemane. I'm standing right next to the tour guide, and he hands me the Bible.

Then he asks me, "Can you read this passage of scripture?"

Now it seemed like it was a long time because every Bible story that I had heard of and even read about when I was a kid crossed in front of me, and I could literally see Jesus at the garden at this moment.

Now, I am a backslidden preacher's kid. I'm drunk and getting ready to read this portion of scripture. I read the scripture and remember a tear forming from my eyes…

Then Jesus came with them to a place called Gethsemane, and said to the disciples, "Sit here while I go and pray over there."

And He took with Him Peter and the two sons of Zebedee, and He began to be sorrowful and deeply distressed.

Then He said to them, "My soul is exceedingly sorrowful, even to death. Stay here and watch with Me."

He went a little farther and fell on His face, and prayed, saying, "O My Father, if it is possible, let this cup pass from Me; nevertheless, not as I will, but as You will."

Then He came to the disciples and found them sleeping, and said to Peter, "What! Could you not watch with Me one hour?

Watch and pray, lest you enter into temptation. The spirit indeed is willing, but the flesh is weak."

Again, a second time, He went away and prayed, saying, "O My Father, if this cup cannot pass away from Me unless I drink it, Your will be done."

And He came and found them asleep again, for their eyes were heavy.

So He left them, went away again, and prayed the third time, saying the same words.

Then He came to His disciples and said to them, "Are you still sleeping and resting? Behold, the hour is at hand, and the Son of Man is being betrayed into the hands of sinners.

Rise, let us be going. See, My betrayer is at hand."

And while He was still speaking, behold, Judas, one of the twelve, with a great multitude with swords and clubs, came from the chief priests and elders of the people.

Now His betrayer had given them a sign, saying, "Whomever I kiss, He is the One; seize Him."

Immediately he went up to Jesus and said, "Greetings, Rabbi!" and kissed Him.

But Jesus said to him, "Friend, why have you come?"

Then they came and laid hands on Jesus and took Him. And suddenly, one of those who were with Jesus stretched out his hand and drew his sword, struck the servant of the high priest, and cut off his ear.

But Jesus said to him, "Put your sword in its place, for all who take the sword will perish by the sword. Or do you think that I cannot now pray to My Father, and He will provide Me with more than twelve legions of angels? How then could the Scriptures be fulfilled, that it must happen thus?"

In that hour Jesus said to the multitudes, "Have you come out, as against a robber, with swords and clubs to take Me? I sat daily with you, teaching in the temple, and you did not seize Me.

But all this was done that the Scriptures of the prophets might be fulfilled." (Matthew 26:36-56 NJKV)

I gave the Bible back to the tour guide and moved all the way to the back of the crowd.

I think my high disappeared because I wasn't feeling excited about being there. We visited Mt Calvary and the tomb where Jesus was crucified and buried. We visited so many Biblical places. We finished the tour and went through all kinds of places in the Holy Land. I remember going back to the ship. I just sat there on my bunk and suddenly, anger rose up in me again.

And those same words came to me again…

"Why did you have to take my dad? Life would be so different if you hadn't taken my dad."

It was a one-way conversation, with me telling all my frustrations to God. So, I continued my life, getting high in the Marine Corps, then coming back to the states. My life was still the same— being angry, getting high, getting drunk and trying to fill this void that I had.

Time went on and I found myself on deployment with a guy who later became one of my best friends. Kent tells me to go with him to Georgia.

I said, "What am I going to do in Georgia?"

Then he said, "There's lots of women in Georgia and you need to come and get you a Georgia peach."

I decided to go to Georgia with him for the weekend. It was everything he said it would be. We would have competitions on who could have the most girls in the room over the weekends. This went on for two to three weekends.

Then on the following weekend (a month later) we went to a football game. It's a small town, so with small towns they make homecoming big. And this was a homecoming weekend.

We were sitting in the bleachers, drunk and high, when all of a sudden, I see a young lady on the track field. She caught my eye. I asked my friend who she was, and he said that he didn't know. So, I didn't pay it any more attention until I saw her again at a gas station.

I was getting out of the car to go buy some cigarettes and I heard somebody make a sound from the car she was in. I turned my head and realized it was her. I walk over to her car and lean into her window.

Then I asked her, "Did you say something?"

She said, "No, I didn't say anything."

Then I said, "Yes, you did. Somebody in this car said something."

I asked her and her friend if they were going to the club, and they said yes. So, I told them we would see them at the club.

My friend Kent, who took me to Georgia, was well known in that town and they had a special parking spot for him right in front of the club. So, everybody is around us and we are getting drunk and high.

Then came in these girls from the gas station walking into the club.

And the one that caught my eye at the football game asked me, "Are you coming in?"

I told her, "Yes, I'll be in in a little bit."

Time went by, and we were still outside, smoking and drinking.

She comes back outside, and says, "I thought you were coming in."

At that same time another young lady started calling my name. Then she asked me if that was my girlfriend.

I told her, "I don't have a girlfriend."

So, we go into the club and start kickin' it. We start dancing and conversating, having a good time. I asked her for her name. Now remember I'm drunk and high and I thought she said Angel. But her name is Angela she says, but they call me Baby Red. We continued dancing and goofing around until closing time of the club. Everybody meets at that same gas station after the club closed and she is getting gas at the pump in front of me. I am pumping gas, and she is pumping gas.

She gets finished before I do and says, "Do you want to kick it tonight?"

I told her yes, so she said, "Follow me."

My car was at the hotel, so I asked my friend, "You have to let me use your car."

Then he said, "Man, don't do it bro, don't do it."

By the time I'm about to get his car, Angela had left. Now I didn't know the town that she was from. So, we get in the car, and we try to go find her. I am doing 90 mph trying to catch up with her. There I was, driving in the dark on winding back roads, trying to catch up to them.

We finally get to the town, and they are nowhere to be found. We drive up and down the town through neighborhoods and still could not find her.

So, we just ended up going back home.

The next day, the same DJ was going to be at the club again. Suddenly, I get a knock on my hotel door. Who was it? It was Angela.

I jumped out of the bed and said, "Wow, how did you find me?"

She just smirked, and we headed to the club and kicked it. I went back to North Carolina that Sunday, tired from the weekend. She had given me her phone number so I would call her during the week.

This ended up growing into a long-distance relationship. I would come down there on the weekends and we would just kick it.

Now she told me that she was 18 years old. I was 20 at the time, so we pretty much had a relationship going on. We met at the end of September and then November was her birthday. I came down on her birthday week. Her family threw her a birthday party. There was a bunch of her family there, and she had a birthday cake.

Soon, everybody said, "Happy 18th birthday!"

At that moment right there, I said, "Wow! I thought you were 18 already!"

We kept meeting every weekend or every other weekend during our long-distance relationship.

I proposed to her on Christmas Eve, and we got married in February. I want to add that her family loves me!

Now on the weekends that I came I was still getting high and drunk, and she did not like that at all. I remember getting on a bus, going from North Carolina to Georgia just to see her.

Leading up to the wedding, I got orders, because our unit was disbanding. I got orders to a new duty station, and I was supposed to leave the week before I got married. I did everything possible to push the days back so I could get married on the day I had scheduled.

On the week of our wedding, I packed my dress blues all of the accessories, and her wedding ring.

I put it all in my suitcase then, my bags went on the bus where the baggage compartment was. We changed buses once or twice.

Once I arrived in Georgia, I was told that my bags had not arrived!

Now I'm stressing, not so much about the ring, but about my uniforms.

They told me that the bag would be on the next bus, but it didn't come until the next day.

So, I went to her house, and we began preparing for

Saturday's wedding. We ordered the cake and the flowers. Everything was ready. Her mom gave me the cake money and told me to hold on to it until Saturday when we picked up the cake.

I told her, "Sure."

The next day, I got a call from the bus station letting me know that my bag was there, but it was in Augusta, GA—74 miles away! So, my mother-in-law's boyfriend at the time and his friend said that they would drive me to the bus station to pick up my bag.

Now these two smoked all the time. ALL the time. They picked me up and we ended up spending all the cake money on marijuana and for 74 miles there and back we smoked up all the cake money.

Once I got home, Angela told me, "I'm done with this. If you don't stop smoking, were not getting married."

I was on Cloud 9, so I said, "Okay, I'll quit."

So, the wedding day arrived, and her mother asked, "Where is the cake money?"

I told her that her boyfriend smoked it up.

She said, "How did he get the money?"

I told her that he got it out of my pocket when I was asleep on the way to pick up my bags. She didn't believe it, and neither did Angela, so it ended up being a pretty rough morning.

Now I am calling my uncle and my family, trying to wire me some money to pay for the cake and I couldn't get a hold of anybody.

Angela said, "I know somebody that could do it, but you have to call and ask for it."

So, I humbly asked this person, and they said yes. Now we have cake at our wedding and everything is prepared.

Now the wedding day has arrived, and all my Marine friends came dressed in their dress blue uniforms and all of

Angela's bridesmaids were dressed in their pretty dresses. Her uncle performed the wedding.

We waited for her dad, who was supposed to give her away, but her dad never showed up. So, her mom's boyfriend at the time walked her down the aisle and gave her away. It was a beautiful ceremony.

We both said, "I do."

Now it was party time!

We were partying, drinking, and having a good time. The family was happy, everything seemed to be going well.

Once everybody headed home, my bride and I had decided to go to a hotel.

But her mother said, "No, you're not. You're not spending any more money. You're going to our house."

So, for our first night as husband and wife, we found ourselves sleeping in her bedroom— in her bed— in her house— with her siblings and her mom in the house.

And that was the first night of married life for Jose and Angela Vargas.

After we got married, we had many ups and downs, many highs and lows. I would say my breaking point came on the day Angela walked up to me, talking about just getting saved and wanting me to get saved, too. I was so mad at the words that had come out of her mouth.

So mad that I just grabbed my can of beer and walked off.

A Change is Coming

I was on barracks duty on this particular Sunday. I went home for lunch and Angela walked into the house with a smile and I knew that there was something different about her. She told me that she gave her life to Jesus and that she was going to serve Jesus with or without me but that she would rather serve Jesus with me. I got so mad that I grabbed a beer and walked out the door. It was an overnight duty, and the TV was left on. I had fallen asleep, when I woke up, I saw Pastor Creflo Dollar on the TV.

He was saying, "Every time the devil reminds you of your past, remind him of his future…"

At that moment, I grabbed the remote and turned the TV off.

A couple of days went by, and I made a phone call to the pastor of the chapel where Angela had gone to church. I was the telephone NCOIC on the base and I threatened to cut off his phones if he did not call my wife and tell her to stop praying. He asked me if I would meet him on Tuesday night at the chapel. I told him I was not going to chapel for service, but he asked if I would be willing to meet him an hour before just to talk. I agreed, so me and my wife pulled up an hour and ten minutes before service started. Attached to the chapel was the 7 Day Store, one of the stores on the base. I went in and bought a carton of cigarettes. Then I pulled out a pack. I was getting ready to smoke in the parking lot of the chapel at the church. At this time, I was smoking a pack of cigarettes a day and drinking 7 to 8 beers a day.

When the pastor pulled up, I was smoking a cigarette. He asked my wife and me to come into the office. He did not judge us. He did not even look at me funny for smoking.

With just a smile on his face, he said, "Come with me to my office."

When we got into the office, we began to talk and conversate, but before I could say much, he was already telling me about myself. He was telling me about a void that I was trying to fill since my father had passed. And that I was trying to fill it with girls, alcohol, and drugs. He began to tell me about the call of God on my life since I was a child—and the destiny God had for me.

At this point, tears were coming down my face. I rededicated my life to the Lord that day. And, you know what? Automatically the taste of alcohol, drugs, and cigarettes, left. I had no cravings for any of them. It left me that day. I haven't had a drink of alcohol or smoked a cigarette or even weed, and I haven't had any cravings since April of 1997.

After that point it still took time for us to heal. So, we joined a local church there on the island of Hawaii and we attended it for 2 years.

We immediately got involved and started off by going to the new foundation classes to learn the Bible. We got involved in different helps ministries at the church. We met other couples. We were looking for friendship because everyone we knew we partied with. We wanted to change our surroundings. So, we started hanging out with church people and we established friendships with them. 25 years later, we still are friends with a few of them. We still communicate and get together with them, even though we are all far apart from each other.

Now, we had never gotten marriage counselling, so we figured things out on our own. There were still arguments. We couldn't talk to a lot of people because we didn't know them like that to trust them. That's where the new foundations class helped us to learn scripture and pray together. It definitely wasn't easy— it was a hard road. But we learned so much along the way. The instructors of the New Foundation Class were Pastors Rodney and Gina Richardson! We are still very close to them today.

I remember a service where the church ministers told the congregation that if anybody wanted to be filled with the Holy Ghost to come up to the altar. The pastor had just preached on the Holy Spirit and speaking in heavenly tongues.

So, I went to the front, and they prayed for me. I know I had gotten filled, but I didn't speak in tongues at that moment, but two days later, while I was in the shower, I started praying and worshipping and suddenly, I started speaking in tongues! This completely changed my prayer life.

On another occasion, a guest speaker came to the church, and he was a prophet.

He called me out and said, "There is a Samuel anointing on you for leadership."

Then he told me, "5 years ago, the enemy had tried to take you out, not once, but twice." Then he put his hands on me and prayed protection over me.

After church, my wife and I went home and calculated 5 years from that day. There were two accidents that we had been involved in during that time. The first accident happened when I was traveling with my family one night and I swerved to miss a deer. The second one we were involved in came so close to being an accident, had I not swerved to miss a car.

We were heading to Georgia from North Carolina on a 4-lane highway. 4 lanes were going north, and 4 lanes were going south. We were in the second inside lane going south. Suddenly, a car came from the northbound lanes and was headed straight to us, to hit us head on. It came from out of nowhere.

I swerved and almost lost control of the vehicle, but I gained control, and we were okay.

So, when the pastor prophesied that to us, it made us think…

Everything he had told us in those moments— it was true. We didn't know anything about the prophetic at this time. How in the world did he know? It was shocking to us. One of those "Wow!" moments.

I realized then that God really had a plan for our lives. Because of that Word, that was the breaking point for us really believing that there was a plan of God for our lives. For somebody that knew nothing about us to talk about an event in our lives that happened 5 years ago…

It blew our minds.

We were like, "Who is this guy?"

At that point I wanted to search deeper into what my calling was.

Shortly after that, I got my rank back. (When I came back from Australia, I had to go to the legal department to talk to a lawyer about getting me out of this adultery case they had on me. I was given NJP (non-judicial punishment) where I lost rank, lost money, and had to do extra duty for the adultery that I had committed).

Our son, Jose Jr. was born during all this change that was going on in our lives. Angela had complications with him as well. She had to go into emergency C-section because he was so big. He came out, weighing 10 pounds and 11 ounces. He was a big one. The clothes that the hospital put on him were so tight. We didn't have to buy our son anything. Everything was provided for him by friends of ours. Our friends from church bought diapers, clothes, car seat, stroller, I mean everything that was needed for him God used our friends to get for him.

Time moved on and before I knew it, I was promoted to

platoon sergeant. Our unit became 99 percent war-ready, and I started having favor in my unit. Things had begun to unfold in our lives after Jose, Jr. was born.

I remember having a series of dreams—3 dreams in 3 nights. In the first dream, I saw my father walking on the stage and up to the pulpit, with the pastor of the church we were attending walking behind him—and I was walking behind the pastor. Then I woke up.

On the second night, I had a dream of my father going to sit down on the stage. The pastor was behind the pulpit, and I was to the side of him. Then I woke up.

On the third night, I'm walking off the stage first, then the pastor was behind me, and my father was nowhere around. So, I called to set up a meeting with the pastor to let him know about my dream to see if he could bring some clarity to it. He told me those were the different stages of my life I had been in.

He said the first dream was my father being my pastor and my leader, the second one was him being my leader and my pastor, and the third one was one day you would have your own ministry.

He asked me if I believed that there was a call of God on my life.

He told me, "I see you going back home to do a work for God there."

I told him, "I do believe it, but I don't want it."

So, he told me that was something I would have to take up with God and that he would help me through it. So, during this stage in my life, I was fighting with God about what He wanted me to do.

From that point, our faith continued to grow and before long, it was time for me to get out of the Marine Corps. I prayed and asked God what my wife and I should do next.

I told the Lord that if I am to stay in the Marine Corps, I

would put in my reenlistment papers to see if they would get approved. So, I put in the reenlistment papers.

Now this is the time when the armed forces were cutting back on reenlistment and enlistments so, because of my NJP, I was denied reenlistment. They had to prepare a severance package for me, and they had to pay me to get out.

My mom had been having trouble in Kansas City and she had prayed, "If Jose would only ask me to come to Hawaii with him…"

Without knowing anything about this, I called her and asked her, "Why don't you come out to Hawaii with me for a little bit?"

So, my mom and my niece came to stay in Hawaii for the last 3 months that I was in the Marine Corps.

During this time my mom was able to minister to me about my marriage without even telling her anything about our situation. She was able to unwind and not think about her problems and I was able to help her while she was helping me.

Before Mom came to Hawaii, she was having problems with my niece. So, we flew to Kansas City to try to help her. I stayed for a week but had to fly back and Angela stayed in Kansas City for a few more days.

While she was there, she went to a revival service with my mom. My wife met the guest evangelist. He was a Puerto Rican from California named Abraham Pedraja.

She told him, "I am married to a Puerto Rican, and he is going to be a preacher one day."

She got his phone number, and I called him from Hawaii. We talked on the phone a few times and established a relationship. He would pray for me on the phone. He would give me counsel on being a man of God.

I had vacation days saved up, so I got out of the Marine Corps early, and went home to Kansas City

We flew from Hawaii to Los Angeles and decided to drive across the country to Kansas City. We had to pick up our car in Long Beach, CA. The person that picked us up from the airport was the evangelist! The same one that I had talked to on the phone but had never seen!

There we were, six of us walking around Los Angeles airport trying to find a bald Puerto Rican evangelist. When we get to the baggage claim, my wife spots him and we meet for the first time. So, there are six of us, each with our own bag. He picks us up in a Volkswagen bug. Bags were all over the top of the car. We even have bags on our laps.

Without him even knowing me, he went out of his way to put us all into his car. He even took us to his home because our car wasn't going to be ready until the next day.

The next day Angela and I got on the road, headed to Kansas City.

CHAPTER 3
Angela

After Jose walked out with the beer, I still had trust issues. I still had a lot of mixed emotions. At this point, I still wanted a divorce. I still hated him. It was like nothing really changed. So, I dealt with a lot of my emotions internally. The good thing about it was I stopped cursing him right away. Even though I felt like cursing him, and even though I felt anger towards him, I stopped cursing. I stopped going out, partying, and going to the clubs.

Jose would come back home almost when it was time to go to bed. He would come home, riding on his bike. He had been drinking. We would sleep on different sides of the bed, and we wouldn't even talk to each other. This went on for at least a week. He would continue on with his regular routine. He would go to work, come home, then take our daughter Kiki to the beach. We were living together and nothing else was happening. We acted just like roommates instead of husband and wife. We went to the beach on the weekend. Monday came, and Jose worked all that day. He didn't come home. Instead, he went to the gym and came home late.

This went on for a week and a half. Then Tuesday came around. On Tuesday, Jose came home for lunch. He told me that he had reached out to the pastor of that church where I gave my life to the Lord.

Then he said, "We have to meet up with the pastor before church."

So, we met him at 6 p.m., because church services started at 7p.m.

When we met with the pastor, he began to tell Jose his whole life story—like it was a book. And then, at that moment, Jose gave his life to the Lord.

After he gave his life to the Lord, there was still a part of me that was angry, but now there was some kind of hope for our marriage. I felt this way because both of us had now given our lives to the Lord. This pastor was also willing to sit and talk to us and help us with some counseling. Since we had never had any kind of counseling before, we decided to give it a try.

Remember the lady at the payphone that I was telling you about earlier? The one that told me that Jesus loved me. Well, she came to my house. She asked me if I would like to go with her husband and her to their church (a different church) on that Sunday.

So, that Sunday morning, we went with this couple to their church. After that service ended, we decided to make that church our home church. And getting there wasn't a short trip, either. This church was way on the other side of the island. It was a 40-minute trip, 4 times a week.

I really liked that church, even though it was farther away than we lived. I enjoyed the worship and the people. I loved the pastor's preaching, and I loved the fellowship. I loved the way that they fellowshipped with each other. We never had that, so I liked it.

One of the services that I had went to was very impactful. I had never seen people falling out. I never experienced dancing or seeing people running to the front worshipping. All of this was very foreign to me— to see people dancing and having a good time at church.

People were happy, so I was drawn to that. Because of my upbringing, I grew up being angry, hostile, and without a father, so when I saw people at church worshipping, I wanted that in my life, too.

There were people coming up to us afterwards, asking if we wanted to fellowship, or go out with them after church. Even though Jose and I still had trust issues with people, we still went to their houses, hung out and had barbeques with people from the church. We did this every week. We hung out with someone from the church every week. Every week we went to a couple's house to eat dinner and to fellowship.

We were never alone.

We didn't realize it, but during those times we were fellowshipping with them, we were learning how to open up that trust and fellowship and have people speak into our lives. Some of them were in ministry and in leadership,

I remember on one occasion when I asked one of the couples if someone could teach me the Bible. I wanted someone to teach me how to live for Jesus. I was told that there was a class on Sunday morning. It was a foundation class that teaches you about the Bible. They also taught the new beginner's classes. I didn't know anything about the Bible at all. I didn't know anything about church ethics or etiquette either because I wasn't brought up in church. I also didn't know anything about the foundation or fundamentals of my relationship with the Lord. Rodney and Gina Richardson were our foundation teachers in that church at that time. I remember going to that class and asking a lot of questions.

One of the things I can remember in the class was in Genesis, Chapter 1—where He was talking about how we were made in God's image. I remember asking questions about that because it caused me to wonder…

"How can I look like a God I have not seen?"

So, the teaching that morning was very interesting. It was so interesting that I couldn't wait for the next Sunday morning class. And this went on for some time. I don't know how long, but it went on until this 5–6-week class ended, and we graduated.

I remember the time when the church was going to do baptisms. I went to the class for several weeks, then I signed up to get baptized, because the announcement was made, and it was coming up in a few weeks. By this time, I was about 6 months pregnant when I got baptized.

I remember walking down to the beach where the baptism

was being held. When I stepped in the water, I was crying. I didn't know what was about to happen. I just remember in my head that something new was about to happen.

Jose, Jr. had been kicking all that day, like something exciting was about to happen. It was almost like a sign of something because the minute I stepped in the water, the baby started kicking with excitement.

I got baptized and when I came up out of the water, I experienced something so real I couldn't believe it. All the hatred, bitterness, pain, and anger towards my husband was gone!

Something came off me, like I was fresh and new. Whatever I had before I went into the water came off me. It was like something was taken off me. And when I walked out of the water and back to the shore, I remember telling Jose that I loved him— after 6 or 7 months of not saying that. Then I told him that I forgave him.

Jose got baptized on the same day that I got baptized. After that, we started to work through all the bitterness, hurt, and pain in our marriage. We had to forgive each other. Then we confessed everything and moved on past it.

Now someone is working with us in our marriage. God really helped our marriage. We had fellowship, connected with counseling, but not actual counseling.

Jose Jr. was born in July of 1998 at Tripler Medical Center in Hawaii. I went in to give birth and found out that I could not have a natural birth. Once again, I would have to have an emergency C-section. The medical team took me to the back, not knowing the baby was 11 pounds. I didn't get to see him at first because I was so drugged up, with all the medicine they gave me when I was giving birth. So, Jose got to see him first. I didn't get to see him until the next day.

When I woke up my husband was holding him, and he was wearing a t-shirt that had Tripler Medical Center on it.

It was a newborn t-shirt, but it looked like a halter top because he was so big.

They had brought clothes to him from the house—because he was so big. The diapers didn't even fit. The lady that told my wife about Jesus (Mama Karen), Ketcha and Dennis (Ketcha and her husband Dennis are a couple that we fellowship with and are Jose Jr.'s godparents) made sure the house was clean. They also made sure everything was ready for the arrival of our son when we got home.

This is when we saw the importance of kingdom friendship. We began to start trusting people because they came to our house when we weren't there, cleaned our house, even went shopping when we weren't there. These were people in our lives that we hung out with every week. We could see our lives beginning to change for the better.

A few months later, there was a Sunday night service, and the power of God was moving tremendously. People were falling out everywhere!

The pastor was walking up and down the aisles holding a handkerchief. I was freaking out about people falling out when he touched them with that handkerchief.

I asked Jose, "Why are people falling out? If all these people are falling out and this is really real, then why am I not falling out?"

The pastor came straight over to me after I said that. As he was coming from the stage, he threw the handkerchief at me. When he did this, I went out in the Spirit, on the concrete floor, still holding the baby in my arms.

As I was holding my newborn baby in my arms, I didn't feel anything. When I woke up, a greeter had my baby in her arms.

I asked her, "What happened to me?"
Then she said, "You got slained in the Holy Spirit."
I said, "The Holy Spirit?"

I told her it felt like I was laying on a bed of feathers—like cotton. It was a soft and relaxing feeling. I was down on that floor for a little while.

I asked her, "How did you get the baby?"

She said, "You got slain in the Spirit, so they took the baby, and I held him."

That was my first encounter with the Holy Spirit.

And so, after that, I was telling one of the ladies I wanted to experience this every time I came to church.

I kept asking her, "If I leave and go home, can I feel the same thing that I felt at church?"

She said, "Yes."

That was the first of many encounters for the next season of our lives.

Shortly after that, Jose's time in the military was coming to an end in Hawaii. And that's when my mother-in-law came to town to help us pack up and get things ready to move to Kansas City.

CHAPTER 4
Jose

We arrived in Kansas City on a Friday. We drove straight there, talking about our family along the way. Then we went straight to my brother's house. I saw that he was preparing for a bible study. What I didn't know was that, while we were in Hawaii having our encounter with the Lord, my family had an encounter with Jesus, and they were all going to the same church. We stayed for the bible study.

Angela

So, the first connection we had was at Jose's brother's house. Since we were going to stay the night there, we connected with some people from the church at the bible study.

Jose

We found out the pastor of the church that my brother was going to and the pastor that picked us up at the airport were friends. So, we visited the church on Sunday.

We attended the church for a few months, and really didn't like it because we were used to a different style of church. The church that we attended in Hawaii had a choir, gospel tracks, and gospel singers—and the church in Kansas City did not.

We went to my mom's church, which was the church that she and my father started and the pastor there was my best friend when we were little kids. It was a Spanish church. The worship was awesome, and the preaching was great. Angela joined the worship team and we both got involved in youth ministry.

We were at that church for a few months, but it started getting hard interpreting the messages from Spanish to English for Angela and our kids.

So, we sat down with the pastor and let him know our concerns. He told us he had been praying for us and God had already told him. So, he recommended a church for us to go to and we visited it the following Sunday.

I remembered that my father had a friend that pastored a church on the Missouri side, and I had not seen him since I joined the Marine Corps. So, we showed up one Sunday morning and after attending a service, fell in love with his church.

At this point, the company that I was working for went bankrupt. So, I wound up changing trades and no longer did communications as a career. Trying to find a job was hard so we decided to talk to our pastor and get some advice from him because we were contemplating moving to Georgia. He had told us to give it a try and see what happens.

So, we were just going to Georgia to search. While we were down there, my wife's aunt said that there was a man at her church that wanted to speak to us.

We met with him and his first question to us was, "What are you doing here in Georgia?"

I told him that we were thinking about moving there.

Then he asked me again…

"What are you doing in Georgia?"

I didn't understand what he was asking me.

So, I told him, "Please explain to me what you are talking about."

So, he begins to tell us that we are not supposed to be in Georgia now. There was work for us to do in Kansas City.

I told him, "There is nothing going on in Kansas City, work wise or anything."

Then he said, "There is work in the kingdom."

We spoke for about an hour.

Then he said, "You need to get back home."

He prayed for us, and we left it at that. About a week

later, I was washing my car at the car wash and saw that same man. He drove by, made a U- turn, then came back to the car wash.

When he came up to me, he asked me, "Why are you still here?"

I told him, "To tell you the truth, I don't have the money to get back home."

Then he pulled out his wallet, gave us $200 and said, "Go home."

The next day we drove back to Kansas City.

To this day, we have never seen this man again. Every time I describe this man, nobody knows him.

I believe he was an angel sent by the Lord—sent to guide us during that season of our lives. During that time, we were still in the healing process of our marriage.

After this took place, we went back to the church we had been attending. We started having family bible studies on Monday nights at my house. My brothers, sisters, and people from the neighborhood would come and God would move tremendously.

I can remember one Saturday at home in Kansas City, when my car broke down. I called my brother and told him that I needed a ride to church on Sunday.

He said, "I'm not driving you all the way to Missouri. You're going to have to go to church with me."

We agreed to go to his church on Sunday morning.

As soon as I walked through the doors, the Holy Spirit told me, "I never told you to leave."

After that, I talked to my pastor and told him what had happened and that we were going back to the church that we first visited. So, we returned and started attending that church and became members of that church.

I clearly remember a service when we did not check in our son to childcare at the church. He stayed in the sanctuary with my sister.

While they were there, she gave him a piece of candy and he started to choke on it and cry. One of the usherettes came and told us we must step out into the foyer because the baby was crying.

We all got up and walked into the foyer. I grabbed my son, checked our daughter out of Kid's Class, and stormed out of the church. One of the church leaders came out behind me.

Then he said, "When you find the perfect church you are looking for, let me know. When you get there, it won't be perfect no more. Because there is no perfect church."

Now I am steaming mad. I looked at him and said, "I have nothing to say, and we walked away."

In my mind, I said, "I would never come back to that church", but when I got home, the Holy Spirit convicted me. I repented and we went back to service that night. Then I apologized to that leader.

Later, we got involved in the church. We were both on the worship team. I was an usher; Angela was an usherette. We were in the Sunday School department where we taught kids, and we helped clean the church.

We were very faithful and committed to the Lord and to leadership. About a year later, we became bible study leaders, and we taught bible studies in our home.

One Saturday during morning prayer at the church, the pastor had all the male bible study leaders come to the side room.

The pastor's wife did the same thing in a different room. I remember the pastor putting a chair in the middle of the room.

Then he said, "If you're battling or struggling with anything, your healing is going to come today."

I was the first one in the chair. I started to speak about how I had committed adultery and carrying the weight of that, and how bad I felt about it. That day all the leaders prayed over me.

I remember the pastor saying, "You have to forgive yourself first."

So, I had to forgive myself for what I had done. That day I felt the peace of God come over me. I felt something lift. The weight that I was carrying for so long lifted off me. I believe that is the day I got freed, delivered, and fully healed from my past. It took a little longer for Angela, so I'll let her tell her side.

Angela

It wasn't as easy for me to let go of the past and trust again, because of the way I grew up. Without having a father figure in my life, and with my mom being so independent, it was kind of the same thing I felt growing up. I had trust issues as a little girl, as a teenager, and now as an adult. It was like something familiar to me, so I said to myself, "I would not trust or hang out with people. I would just stay to myself."

At the church we were serving in, the pastor told me that I needed to let go, trust again and make friends.

Then I asked him, "So how do I do that?"

And he said, "You're just going to have to trust again."

Then I asked him, "How could I do that?"

He said, "Start out by fellowshipping, going out, and having a cup of coffee with your fellow church members."

The very first time we went to fellowship, we went to the pastor's house and his wife made waffles for all of us. We sat and fellowshipped and talked. She made the best waffles with peanut butter and honey topping —and we had a cup of coffee. I really enjoyed myself. She did this often.

So that night, it felt good to fellowship with people

because they were genuine, just to laugh and eat dinner with people. I started opening myself up and the walls started coming down that I had built around myself for so long.

Then I remembered there was a weekend when another couple came and asked if I would go with them to get coffee. I ended up going, and after that I went out to get coffee with another couple from the church. More walls came down and I began to be a little more comfortable with leaders from the church. This went on for a while.

One Saturday morning at prayer, I remember telling the Lord, "Help me to trust again."

And every Saturday, I would meet at church for prayer and there were leaders there that would teach me how to pray and with time, I realized that God was delivering me from all the hurt and trust issues from my marriage. I had gotten over bitterness, so now I was ready for this new journey that God was taking me on— the next steps of my life.

Jose

Through that process, God has used us to help marriages that have gone through similar situations like we have gone through. We have been able to speak into their lives, marriages have been restored and where once divorce was the word spoken in the home, now reconciliation was happening.

We were part of revivals that were scheduled for 3 days but ended up lasting for 12 weeks. I remember one all-night prayer meeting that we had. The church was broken up into different teams for bible study. It was 1 a.m. and it was our team's turn to lead in prayer.

I remember being prostate on the altar when I heard the Holy Spirit tell me," Do you still want to know why I took your father?"

And I said, "Of course I do."

I would always ask God, "Why couldn't He take a drug dealer, drug addict, prostitute or a sinner off the streets instead of my father?"

During this prayer meeting, He answered that question for me.

He said to me, "You selfish young man. Your father was ready to be with me. If I had taken one of those you wanted Me to take, their hope of salvation would be gone at that moment. But your father would be with Me. There are lots in this world that are not ready, and I've called you to make a difference in their lives."

I got up from the altar at that moment and repented and since that day, I have not asked that question to God again.

As time moved on, the gift of the evangelist was burning inside of us— to want to go and preach to the lost. That they would get saved and know Jesus.

CHAPTER 5
The Ordination

Jose

In the end of 2004, Prophet Rob Sanchez came to our church to preach a revival. He called my wife and I out to come to the front.

He begins to give us a Word and he asked us if we were done having babies.

We had a boy and a girl, so we thought we were complete. So, we told him, "Yes, we're done."

Then he said, "I see a little girl with long black curly hair that will travel with you and will bring joy to your home. She will not lack anything. Everything will be provided for her."

The church went crazy, yelling and screaming, but my wife had tears. Emotions got the best of her. She was hysterically blown away. We thought that we were done. There was no planning for her.

Shortly after, I started traveling with my pastor at that time, being his armorbearer. On the trips, he would talk to other pastors (at that time) to allow me to minister at their church and this went on for a period of time. I met a lot of preachers and gleaned and learned from a lot of them on these trips. I was preaching a revival in San Antonio, TX. After the last night of the revival, I went back to my hotel room and called my wife to tell her how the services went at the revival. The church back home in Kansas City was also having a revival with another evangelist. So, we were going back and forth, talking about how great both revivals were going.

Then all of a sudden, Angela tells me, "I have something to tell you…I'm pregnant."

We were so excited about the pregnancy.

In July of 2005, I was ordained as an evangelist, and I started walking in that office. Angela went with me on a few trips, but because of our kids being young and her being pregnant with our baby girl, she was not able to travel as much.

In September of 2005, we welcomed our baby girl, Marisol into the world.

Out of the three births this one was the smoothest and exactly how Prophet Rob had prophesized. She has long black curly hair, she brings joy to our house, she travels with us, and all her needs have been met.

When Marisol was 4 years old her hair began to fall out in chunks. She lost her eyebrows, and she lost pigmentation on her right ankle. We took her to the doctor and found out that she had Alopecia and Vitiligo on her right leg. They wanted to give her shots in her head and other treatments, but we told the doctors no. They sent her to a dietician. They sent her to a hair specialist and a dermatologist. Nothing seemed to help. She would walk around with a headband covering the bald spots on her head. On her first day of kindergarten her headband started sliding down where it made her self-conscious, and insecure about herself. We would post scriptures of healing all around her bedroom on the walls. And we would pray with her for healing. One day she asked if she could call Pastor Rob so that he could pray for her over the phone.

Angela

So, we called Prophet Rob and he prayed for her. He prophesied to her over the phone and told her that her hair was going to grow back and be strong. She was 7 years old. She came to me and told me she had a dream. She was super excited telling me the dream. I asked her to tell me about the dream. She said that the Lord spoke to her in her dream and told her that He was going to heal her.

After hearing that, I started crying, and I said, "Wow." I asked her if she believed that God was going to heal her, and she said yes. So, every day, she would go to the mirror to see if her hair was growing. In her bedroom she had a closet door that was a full mirror, so she would go there every day and look at her eyebrows and hair— every day.

One day, Jose and I were sitting downstairs.

Marisol ran downstairs and said, "Hey guys, you are not going to believe this!"

She said that there were hairs on her eyebrows and that her eyebrows were growing back! We were sitting there listening, crying, excited, and happy. Looking at Marisol, it was like something that she really truly believed— that God had healed her because every time something would happen, she would be happy. We would continue waiting for the full manifestation of her healing. She did not doubt at any time.

Jose

But even in this, it helped grow our faith, especially in healing. At 8, her faith and belief that God was going to heal her increased over the years, that by the time her 10th birthday came around, she was completely healed.

Angela

It was a full manifestation of Marisol's healing. The doctors said it was a miracle. The doctor said in all his years of practice, he had never seen someone's hair grow without hair injections or medications.

Jose

The doctors were blown away after her healing. She never had to go back to any hair specialists or anything like that.

After Marisol's miraculous healing, Angela and I evangelized for another year, did several revivals, and preached in different states. We saw signs, wonders, and miracles. I remember being in Dallas, Texas, doing the Dallas tour. We were preaching in Dallas, Austin, San Antonio, then back to Dallas. While we were in Dallas, we got a phone call from our pastor (at that time). He said that he needed us to come home because he was given another church. We came home and Angela and I really prayed about this next move. We went to the pastor's office and told him we were willing to put our evangelist calling on the shelf and help him pastor this other church. He told us he wasn't going to make us do anything—this would be a decision we would have to make.

We had already prayed and felt the peace of God, so we decided to help build the church. We became campus pastors of one church in two locations. We learned so much about being assistant pastors/campus pastors. We were so honored to serve as campus pastors and assistant pastors at both locations.

I thought I would be a campus pastor for 2 years but ended up being campus pastor for 8 years. During those years, I worked at the church office on the administration side of the church. I began to learn that side of ministry. Angela always had a part, because she was campus pastor with me, and she was assistant pastor as well.

During that time, the church purchased a school. There was a need for a principal, so I was asked to cover that position.

For one school year, I was the principal. Angela would come and help at the school with the lunchroom and cleaning. Now I was the principal, still the campus pastor, assistant pastor, and executive pastor of the office–all at one time. Don't ask me how that happened, but it happened. We wore many hats, and we knew which role to step into and which hat to put on in the various ministries.

Angela

By the grace of God, we were allowed to do all these ministries. In every title that we held— God graced us to be effective in each one.

As a wife in ministry, with all the training and the serving, it taught me to really rely on the Holy Spirit for help. It is impossible to do those many ministries without the Holy Spirit leading and guiding you.

I was a wife, a mother, and serving in ministry full-time. Ministry is not for the faint at heart, but it is rewarding. I was learning to prioritize my life. The most important thing was my relationship with the Lord and keeping Him first and He gave me the strength to do it.

I would get up at 4 a.m. in the morning to go to work. I would get off between 1:30 and 2 pm and I would go home and cook dinner and take care of my family. I would get dressed for church services and be at church an hour before to prepare for the service. Then I would stay after service for fellowship, any counseling or administration stuff. I would get home at 11:30-midnight, then do it all over again. It went on this way for over 10 years. I lived that kind of lifestyle.

I found a lot of my encouragement in serving and loving God's people. I found my strength during the times I was weak. God would give me the strength to minister and encourage others. God gave me the most strength when I was the weakest. Many times, I felt like giving up, but God gave me strength to continue.

To this day, I am still ministering, still preaching.

One of the most important things that I realized in everything that I have done in ministry is allowing God to be my focus. To fall in love with Him daily. The more I learned to love God, the more I knew who the Lord was, the eager I was to do more for Him to serve His people. In all of this, the Lord graced us to do it. It is impossible to be spiritually healthy in ministry, serving and dealing with people without the Holy Spirit. It is truly impossible.

We always made family time a priority. We always told our kids that they were our first ministry. They are our first disciples, and church was always second to them. Just in that, it kept our family a very close-knit family. God is about family, and He's about families in the church.

Our kids were in sports, but the sports were outside of church events. All our kids did sports growing up, but we didn't allow it to affect ministry.

We always say, "God is first, family is second, and church is third."

As long as we keep those things in order, our God will truly grace us.

We have always had dinner at the dinner table—as a family. Even while I traveled, the kids still sat at the dinner table. We always snacked or ate something until Dad got home. Everything we did we did with our kids. Family was a priority. So, if God can trust you with your family, He can trust you with His church family.

Jose

We made lots of mistakes and had lots of failures in those ministry roles that we held, but we learned what to do and what not to do and how to do it and how not to do it.

Angela

We learned how to balance family life and ministry.

It seemed like when we finally thought we had got it, God would ask something else of us as far as ministry was concerned.

If you are faithful with little, God will make you rulers of much...

He who is faithful in what is least is faithful also in much; and he who is unjust in what is least is unjust also in much.
(Luke 16:10 NKJV)

CHAPTER 6
A New Season of Ministry

Around 2014 we had a meeting with our pastors and told them that we wanted to be sent out to start a church in Atlanta, Georgia.

His reply was "Yes, we will send you out, but we won't send you out of this year's conference."

So, the plan was to be sent out in 2015 to start a church in Georgia.

In November of 2014, the pastor came into my office and told me that there was a change of plans. He said that he needed us to take over a church in Independence, Missouri.

I asked him, "What about Georgia?"

He replied, "Georgia will have to wait."

So, Angela and I took over the church in November of 2014. Like any transition, it was challenging, but we were ready to step into the next transition that God had set for us. The church had about 30 members, but they all loved God. We started training, discipling, and building up couples to step into their God-given assignments.

We changed a lot of the look of the church to make it fit us— and started having church services where God would move supernaturally. People would come walking down the street, then walk into our church service and get radically saved. Young people would see people walking down the street, then go out there and bring them into the church. We did community outreaches where we fed the homeless and took food and hygiene necessities. We saw the church grow in numbers. We went from 30-40 members to 100 members in 6 months.

We were renting a building for our church services and when it rained, the rain would come down from the ceiling tiles, so we had to rearrange the sanctuary. We had everybody sit on the side that was not wet. During all of that, nobody complained.

Visitors still came and souls were being added to the

kingdom. Because of the condition of the building, we were pretty much forced to look for another building, because we had outgrown it for our church services.

We now had Sunday services, standing room only, and our children's ministry was packed with children.

Angela

We had some God moments in that building. There was a guy who had been homeless for quite a few years. He lived in a tent in the park across the street from the church.

One Saturday morning, he walked over during a prayer meeting and asked if he could get some help. We prayed for him. He gave his life to the Lord that same day. When he came back to church the next day, we did not even recognize him. One of our leaders from the church took him to get something to eat, then to a place where he could get a shower, get his hair cut, and get some clothes. From that date forward, he started coming to the church every week to help with anything the church needed done. He became a faithful member of the church.

We had an Easter outreach and wanted to reserve the park for our Easter egg hunt. The city said that it was on a first come, first serve basis.

So, that young man said, "I will put my tent up over here and start setting up, first thing in the morning, because I live here."

We had over 300 people show up to that Easter egg event. God continued to bring men and women like him into our church. There were some good revivals in that building. Some great ministers came through and preached some revivals, and people would get saved and locked in. The church continued to grow.

Jose

We were in the process of finding a new building. So, we talked to our pastor at the time and told him about what was happening in our church. He thought of an idea that would help both of us.

He said, "Let's merge your church with the church that you used to be the campus pastor at. You'll move your congregation to that building and you will pastor both congregations in that building."

My wife and I prayed about it, and we said, "Okay, let's do it."

In July 2015, we merged both churches together and I became the senior pastor of the church. Not only that, but our children were also involved in ministry. Our oldest daughter Kianna was the worship leader, Jose Jr, was part of the youth leadership and helped in audio visual department and our youngest, Marisol, helped in the children's ministry. They were very active and faithful in their roles.

It definitely was not easy, merging a city church with a suburban church. It was two different lifestyles, two different people groups. There was lots of friction, but God was definitely in it.

We had a mighty move of God and the church continued to grow. We had multiple revivals where signs, wonders, and miracles happened. We had community outreaches where we gave goodie bags to every police officer and fireman in the city. We did community events where the fire chief and police chief came out to be a part of the events.

The church went through some ups and downs for a period of time. We lost people and we gained people, but the Word continued to be preached. We still had visitors come and get saved. Revival was still happening, and the church was still growing.

In 2016, we met with a couple that had a call of God on their lives to pastor a church. I took the young man with me to a church planting conference in California and he was so inspired. He wanted to be sent out to start a church.

I asked him what city he wanted to go to, and he said, "St Louis, MO."

We prayed together, then went to visit the city together. We came back and talked to our pastor at the time. In July of 2016 we sent him, his wife, and family to start a church in St. Louis, MO.

We are so proud of this couple for saying "Yes" to God. They are doing a great job there in St. Louis, reaching the lost and winning souls for the kingdom.

Early in 2017 God had spoken to me to give up my church and return to evangelizing. I fought with God.

I said, "We are in revival. Why would I go and do that?"

Four months later, God spoke to me again and said, "Give up your church and go back to being an evangelist."

I thought I would be smart and negotiate with God and I told Him I would pastor and evangelize at the same time.

But He said, "No, give up your church, and be a full-time evangelist."

So, in September of 2017, we gave up our church and became full-time evangelists, not knowing what to expect. But we believed that if God called us, He would provide for us. So, we moved to Georgia to have our ministry based in Georgia.

Angela

During that time, we didn't spend much time in Georgia. We were spending so much time on the road, going from church to church and for one whole year, we were preaching more than when we were in Georgia.

During the time we spent in Georgia, our two oldest kids were still living in Kansas. Both of our kids (Kianna and Jose, Jr.) walked away from the things of God.

They got into drugs and alcohol and their lives were spiraling downward. It had gotten to the point where we would cry out to God.

We wondered, "How can God use us to save so many, then we lose our own children to the world? Because of the kids falling away, we were pulled to come back to Kansas City to help restore them.

While we were still living in Georgia, we had gotten an invitation to come and preach in Liberty, MO and the pastor asked us to send a picture for the flyer. So, we took a picture on the porch, and I sent the picture to the pastor, and I heard the Spirit of the Lord say, "I'm up to something." And I responded, "You are always up to something."

He said, "But this time I am up to something."

So, from that day forward, we put the phrase, "God is Up to Something" on everything because He was up to something in everything we did. We have "God is Up to Something" merchandise that has traveled not only in America, but to other countries.

During this season of trials with our two older kids, God was still using us in signs, wonders, and miracles as we traveled.

We saw God heal a woman of cancer and do restoration on marriages. We saw healings, miracles, and multiple souls coming to the Lord. We saw the hand of God moving in our finances. The evidence of the Holy Spirit was in every service.

I was preaching a revival at Huntington Park, CA, and was doing an altar call. People were coming up for salvation. Then we began to minister over people individually. Angela called out a big usher from way in the back of the room. This was a big, tatted up man, and she began to prophesy over him, telling him he was big and bad on the outside, but inside he was a big teddy bear. I am looking around for other ushers, just in case something went down they would be ready, but the power of God hit him as he was walking towards the altar. He fell down at the altar, crying.

Things like that happened at every one of our services, by the prophetic words of our ministry. The power of God would save, heal, and deliver. For one whole year, we traveled. Out of 52 weeks, we were gone for 40 of them. We were on the road, going from hotel to hotel, church to church. In that first year we flew just a few times, but most of the time we drove to different cities. We traveled with one suitcase each, and our baby girl on our side.

The Bible says, *"The steps of the righteous are ordered by the Lord,"* and He ordered our steps for that season. We were not in need of anything because He had provided for it all...

We established new relationships with different pastors as we traveled. Before we knew it, our ministry had expanded internationally. We were able to go to Nicaragua, Peru, and different parts of Mexico. Those relationships opened new doors for us.

I remember doing an anniversary service in Michoacan, Mexico. God was moving tremendously when a lady came up for prayer that had a huge stomach in which she looked pregnant. I asked her how many months she was. She responded that she was not pregnant, but she had a large mass in her stomach and did not have the money to go to the doctor. I asked her if she believed that God could heal her, and she said yes! I laid hands on her and immediately she fell to the ground. I told the usherette not to lay a blanket over her. Her stomach began to go down and the mass disappeared. The next day she returned and testified how God healed her. She brought other family members and they got saved.

On another occasion I was privileged to travel to Trujillo, Peru with a team. I was scheduled to minister on Wednesday night. I called up anyone that was sick or hurt to come up to the stage. Some people came up and got healed of back pain, knee pain, and foot pain. There was a young lady that came up and could not talk. She had just gotten out of the hospital and came straight to the service. The doctor had just told her that her vocal cords were bad. She was a worshipper and was upset that the doctor said she could not sing anymore. I asked her if she believed that God could heal her, and she said yes! I laid my hands on her throat, and she went down to the ground. I asked the ushers to pick her up. I asked her what happened to her. She said that she felt a warm sensation go through her neck and throat area. I asked if she would grab the mic and just talk. Not only did she talk, but she started singing. She was completely healed that night.

On another occasion we were in Tijuana, Mexico preaching at a conference. We called people up that needed a miracle. We began to pray for the people that needed a miracle. A young lady came up for prayer that had Scoliosis and was in extreme pain. During the alter call, I said that God was healing somebody with extreme back pain. After the service, she came to Angela and I and said that she was the one with extreme back pain. She showed us a picture of her spine before that night and then showed us how her back was now straight. She got healed that night and has been witnessing in her region about the power of God. She messaged us a week later and told us that God had restored her relationship with her father. She had not seen or talked to her father in 2 years because she was angry and hated him. She asked him to forgive her, and she was able to meet her little sister for the first time. She sent us a video of the meeting at the airport as she embraced her father and tears rolling down both of their faces. God is so good!

Our ministry was expanding, and God was up to something.

CHAPTER 7
The Pandemic

In March of 2020, we were in Lancaster, Pennsylvania preaching some meetings. God moved tremendously in those services. New relationships were established and now it was time to head back home. We were supposed to fly home on Monday morning. But we got an alert from the airline that they changed our flight. So, we got to the airport and found out that our flight had changed again. We traveled from Harrisburg, Pennsylvania to Chicago, Illinois and in Chicago our flight got changed again. We finally arrived in Kansas City on that same night.

Our biggest fear was we were not going to make it home, due to so many flight changes and the news of the pandemic that had begun to blanket the entire world.

The next day, our country shut down.

The way that we did life totally changed for everyone.

My wife and I are itinerant ministers, traveling from place to place. That's how we made our living. In 72 hours, all our summer speaking engagements had gotten cancelled.

So now we are in deep prayer, talking to God and asking, "What is next?"

I remember praying one morning and God told me to preach. I told Him, "You open the door, and I will preach but all the churches are closed right now."

So, God told me, "I've given you an open door. It's called the internet. Now go and preach."

So, my wife and I set up our iPhones on our dining room table. We had morning devotionals and prayer, 7 days a week for 2 months.

Our ministry started to get known from Facebook live. Our online presence grew so we wanted to make it better.

We had a spare bedroom I was using as an office. I suggested that we convert it into a studio. We didn't have a lot of finances, so we used our iPhones, a couple of photography lights, and a computer. We started doing viral revivals in the evening time and we would preach revival services online every night. Pastors would contact us, asking us to do revivals on their platforms on social media.

I remember God telling me, "I told you I was up to something."

People started supporting our ministry on a monthly basis. We were able to buy a camera, get better lighting, and a better computer, which improved the quality of our videos. We continued the morning devotions and viral revivals for months.

Our online viewership increased even to locations like Hong Kong, the United Kingdom, Australia, the Philippines, even the Middle East and Mexico, just to name a few. We had testimonies of people getting healed supernaturally in their homes.

Angela

Marriages were restored, and some people who had been dealing with mental illness (because of being closed in due to the pandemic) found healing because of prayer and worship. One lady came across our site and said it helped her. She had been going through a lot in her marriage. She said they would wait every morning to view us during that time of their life.

A lot of people were not able to physically work, so they watched the service. They believed God for their healings and miracles. If we missed an airing, people would inbox us, asking if we would be coming on that day because the ministry was so encouraging.

Jose

We experienced salvations during the viral revivals, and even through the airwaves God used us in signs, wonders, and miracles. Prophetic words would go through us to other pastors during Zoom meetings that they had with us that would alter the destiny of their churches. We were asked to record some of our messages from our studio so they could play them on their platforms on Sunday mornings. For some, the pandemic was a bad thing, but for us it was a good thing, because it launched our ministry to where it is today.

For example, we were able to re-establish our relationship with our foundation class instructors, Pastors Rodney and Gina Richardson, from the church that we attended in Hawaii. We were able to go spend Memorial Day 2020 in Aurora, Colorado. They have been instrumental in our ministry. We have ministered at their church numerous times and our relationship has gotten even closer. We appreciate relationships like that, those people that tell you what you need to hear, not just what you want to hear.

Also, more funding started coming in for our ministry where we were able to buy more equipment. We moved our studio from our spare bedroom into the basement of our house. Our basement was bigger and not really being used. We set it up where we had two different sets. One set was for morning devo and the other set was for viral revival. We would move the cameras and lightning around, depending on which set we were going to use in that segment. We learned a lot of camera positioning and a bunch of what to do and what not to do on camera. It was a learning experience that, if it wasn't for the pandemic, we would not have learned.

God continued to bless and expand our ministry.

We did numerous outdoor services where people stayed

in their cars, and we preached from an open trailer. You would hear car horns going off for "Amens" and as people drove off, we would put our hands on the car and pray for families as they drove off. We had to adapt and overcome to continue preaching the gospel by all means necessary.

By August churches started opening again. Now we were able to travel once again. We went to some churches and many people came to us telling us how our ministry helped them during the pandemic.

People would come to us and tell us, "We see you every morning. We don't miss a single morning."

Some said, "We got saved during your viral revivals."

Others would say, "We got healed during one of your online services."

And these are the types of testimonies we received when we got back on the road.

We continued our morning devo and viral revival when we were not on the road, but our hearts have always been to be on the road and face to face with people so we could physically lay hands on them. New relationships were established during this season of our lives. Our intimacy with God rose to another level. Our relationship with our children got stronger.

Angela

Even when times of discouragement would try to settle in from not traveling on the road, we found strength in the Lord. We encouraged ourselves by reaching out and preaching to others. We've always said every day is a day of opportunity. You get a choice and a chance to make a difference in someone's life. A lot of our encouragement came from the preaching and teaching. We spent a lot of time ministering and talking to our kids because they

CHAPTER 8
God is Up to Something!

I'm reminded of a part of the old hymn by the late Bishop G.E. Patterson, "When I think of the goodness of Jesus and all that he has done for me; my soul cries out Hallelujah I thank God for saving me." As I look back over seasons in our marriage, ministry, and even life; I thank God that he didn't give up on us. We have had a lot of ups and downs. We have had a lot of learning seasons and we have had a lot of hard knocks on the road. I just thank God that he has entrusted us with the ministry we have and the ministries that we have been privileged to be a part of. We have had great leaders in our lives. We have had great mentors to help guide us and teach us and encourage us in difficult times. I thank God that he has chosen us and has found us faithful in all that we have put our hands to do. It has not been easy, but it sure has been rewarding. In what way do you ask? To see somebody's marriage about to be destroyed by the enemy and see God step in and restore what could have been lost is a great feeling. To see somebody that was heading to destruction of their life by drugs and alcohol and to see the hand of God deliver and set them free is amazing. To see somebody's children or spouse come to the Lord after years of praying and believing that God would bring them back is a feeling that you will never forget. To see bodies healed of cancer, tumors, back pains, knee pains, hearing loss, and so many other pains and diseases and infirmities builds up your faith. Testimonies like this and so many others are the reward we get to receive by saying yes to ministry. Yes, it is hard, and it is not for the faint of heart but when you can experience this in your own life and get to see it manifest in other people's life, there is no greater reward than that.

We realized that God has always been up to something in our lives, marriage, ministry, children, and every step of faith we have taken.

I often think to myself, what if I never went to Georgia

with Kent or what if I never went on that Holy Land tour while in Israel. What if Angela never went to that small chapel on Marine Corps Base Hawaii. What if Angela and I never agreed to meet with the pastor from the chapel on the base. Everything happens for a reason. God's timing is very precise, and we might not understand why things happen the way they do or even the events that happen throughout your life but know that God is always up to something. He was up to something when Angela and I first met, and I am so glad He hasn't stopped being up to something.

2022 brought yet another change into our story. After serving God and the leadership of the church we were attending for 22 years, God moved us from there into another chapter.

We thank the pastors and the leadership for the opportunities given to us while under their leadership. May the Lord bless and keep you.

God has recently moved us to be joined to the *Better Together Network* under the leadership of Bishop Joey and Pastor Meredith Zamora. We are so looking forward to this next chapter in our life.

We are still traveling and preaching the gospel of Jesus Christ in churches as well as being conference speakers. Our God is up to something merchandise is still a big conversation starter everywhere we go. We go to the store and people are asking how to get one. We were at the airport in Pheonix, AZ and a lady asked us how to get one. We gave her the information and she ordered a shirt for her and her husband. We have been privileged to minister throughout the United States and in countries such as Peru, Nicaragua, Hong Kong, and Mexico. We have seen God do signs, wonders, and miracles in our meetings. We have seen marriages restored, bodies healed, destinies altered, and lives saved and added to the Kingdom of God. We have had the awesome privilege of discipling men and women to become pastors and great leaders. We have seen firsthand; God heal vocal cords and see tumors disappear. We have seen people in wheelchairs come out of their wheelchairs and begin to walk. God has been so good to us. Even when we were not good to ourselves or to each other, He was still good to us. Our children are all saved and in ministry. We are so thankful to the Lord for that. We can honestly say that if it wasn't for The Lord on our side, where would we be?

2022 ended with celebration and grief...

Our son Jose Jr. got married to his girlfriend Aaliyah on December 17, and Angela's family was able to make the trip from Georgia. Angela's mother, sick and all, made the trip, and we were able to laugh and love on her during the few days she was with us. On December 27, Angela's mother went to be with the Lord. Angela had the awesome privilege of leading her mom to the Lord while she was in Kansas City for our son's wedding.

Where we are now...

2023 brought yet another chapter into our lives. After prayerfully seeking God for the next direction for our ministry, and speaking and receiving counsel from our Pastors, God spoke to us yet once again to move to Georgia and start a church. This is something that I did not want to do again. God had spoken to Angela a year ago that we would be moving back to Georgia, but she had told God that he would have to speak to me himself. That He did do, and He spoke it very clearly. God gave us the city, the area, and the surrounding landmarks as to where we were to live. This was a miraculous move. When I say miraculous, that is what

I mean.

When God spoke to us to move from Kansas City to Georgia, we had $48 in our account. I told God that He was really going to have to be up to something for this one! God has such a great sense of humor! We went to Georgia to spend Mother's Day with Angela's family. While we were there, we went off to look for a house for us to move into in a few months. We spent 3 days just looking for a house to call home. We thought we had found the right one, but it fell through. We headed back to Kansas City to begin packing our house for the move. Did I mention that we only had $48 in our bank account? We needed $13,000 just to move. That was truck rental, first month's rent, deposit, bills in Kansas City so we can leave with a clean slate, and other expenses that were needed. Can I tell you that within 1 week God provided every dime we needed to move. We found the house that we wanted and in 3 days we got approved to move in. When God is up to something, I mean He is up to something.

There is one thing that I have learned in my walk with God and that is that when heaven has a plan for you, come hell or high water, you can't be stopped!

We moved to Georgia in July of 2023 and have been living under an open heaven of God's favor. We are in the process of launching Re-Church. God gave me the name sitting in church service on one Sunday morning and He told me that it is time for His Church to return or do again Church the way He initiated it to be.

He gave me these 5 statements which are our church's mission statement:

1. Revive your Faith.
2. Renew your Mind.
3. Refresh your Worship.

4. Restore your Relationship.
5. Replenish your Strength.

We are so excited about this next move in our lives. We are up for the challenge. Everything we went through in our lives and ministry has prepared us for this season of our lives.

Our two daughters and grandson made the move with us to Georgia. Our son Jose Jr and his wife Aaliyah stayed back in Kansas City doing ministry at the church where they serve. Seeing our kids serving God at the capacity that they do brings so much satisfaction to us and it makes it all worth the pain, pressure, and late-night prayers added with tears and fasting.

I heard a sermon not long ago titled, "It's worth the wait!" I will say that yes, it is worth the wait. No matter what happens in life, we win because we are Kingdom winners.

If we can encourage you in any way while reading our story is this…

God is up to something!

Made in United States
Troutdale, OR
09/07/2023

12703007R00054